I-SPY

with David Bellamy

AT THE ART GALLERY

I-Spy Books
12 Star Road, Partridge Green
Horsham, Sussex RH13 8RA

Okay for those who live in London or other big towns, but what about me out here in the sticks or the suburbs? Well, you may be surprised to find just how close you have a local art gallery or collection in your museum, library or even school.

Art galleries are marvellous quiet places where you can sit and gaze to your heart's content at scenes of your local landscape, even perhaps your village street painted centuries ago.

I, however, warn you that once you have become hooked on I-SPYING in art galleries you will be hooked for life!

SCORING

As you spot each of the paintings pictured here—and answer the simple question—you earn an I-SPY score. When your scores total 1250 you may award yourself the rank of ART OBSERVER with Silver Honours. When they reach a complete total of 1500 points you are entitled to the rank of ART OBSERVER with Gold Honours; you may then send your book to me, and I shall return it to you stamped with my personal seal. Your certificate of rank is on the inside-back-cover of this book.
Good hunting!

This book is about pictures painted in Europe between the years 1200 and 1900 AD. It does not deal with art of this century, so search out pictures that are about 100 or more years old.

As well as in galleries and museums, you can find paintings in country houses and churches, and you may score points for those. You can also use this book if you go on holiday abroad. You may NOT score points for pictures seen in books, or for prints; you must find THE REAL THING!

Old paintings are very delicate. Some art galleries put glass over them to protect them; others don't, as glass sometimes makes it difficult to see the picture properly. But whether there is glass over the picture or not, it is very important to remember never to touch it.

Stubbs: Cheetah and Stag with Two Indians

HOW TO READ A LABEL

(But when you are in an art gallery try to read the labels as little as possible. It's much more important to spend the time looking at the paintings!)

Most art galleries and museums label their exhibits to give you information. A label on a painting will usually tell you the name of the artist and the title of the picture, and it may also say when the picture was painted and give the years of the artist's birth and death.

It may say, for example, British School or Italian School. This just tells you the country he worked in—it has nothing to do with schools as you know them! And don't be surprised if the first thing on the label is a number. This will just be part of the gallery's way of numbering its pictures as it gets them.

The label on a very famous painting in the National Gallery, London, reads as follows:

1207 THE HAY-WAIN (1821)
BY CONSTABLE 1776-1837 BRITISH SCHOOL

See if you can work out what it is all about.

Murillo: Self Portrait

SELF PORTRAIT

A self portrait is just what it sounds like: a picture of the artist done by him, or her self. Sometimes a painter will be shown holding a palette and brush, or something else which tells us a bit more about the artist's life. Often the artist stares straight out of the painting because he would have been looking in a mirror to get a true likeness. (See also p.39)

Whose self portrait did you find?..

What else was in the painting?...

....Score **40**

Van der Goes: Sir Edward Bonkil in Adoration

DONOR PORTRAIT

Long ago, rich people would pay artists to paint pictures to be put in their local church. They might do this because they had come through some illness or other difficulty and wanted to show God how grateful they were; or because they thought it would help to get them to Heaven when they died. The picture would be a holy one, usually showing Mary and Jesus and maybe a few saints. Sometimes the donor (the person who gave, or donated, the picture) would be included in it, either alone or with his family. Look out for a well-dressed person who does not look like a saint, kneeling at the front of the picture.

Was your donor painted larger or smaller than the Holy people?..

Was the donor's family included?................................

Who was the artist?..

Where was the painting?.......................Score **50**

Gainsborough: The Morning Walk

MARRIAGE PORTRAIT

Nowadays, newly married couples often like to have their photograph taken. Before photography was invented, well-off couples might have their picture painted. This would not usually show the actual ceremony or wedding party, but would be of the couple indoors or out of doors in their every-day surroundings. The picture's label will probably not tell you that it is a marriage portrait, but any portrait of a young married couple is likely to be one. The picture will not include anyone else.

Was your couple indoors or outside? ....

Were they sitting or standing? ....

Did they look happy? ....

In which gallery did you see the painting? ....

....

Who was the artist? .... Score **50**

Hals: A Family Group in a Landscape

GROUP PORTRAIT

A group portrait shows a number of people who have a special relationship with each other, like a company of soldiers, or a family. Or it may commemorate a special occasion, like a peace treaty being signed or an exhibition being opened. Sometimes there is a key to show who everyone is.

What sort of people were in your group portrait?..............

....

Was a special occasion shown, and if so, what?..............

....

Who painted it?...
Where did you see the picture?...

....Score **30**

Reynolds: Miss Bowles

PORTRAIT OF A CHILD

Of course you find portraits of children in a family group, but to score your points you must find a portrait of a child on its own.

Was the child in your portrait larger than life, smaller than life, or about life size?..
How old did he or she look?..
Was he or she shown with anything to play with? If so, say what..
Write the artist's name..
Did the label tell you the child's name, too?..
.... Score **30**

Gheeraerts the Younger: Elizabeth I

PORTRAIT OF A KING OR QUEEN

Long ago, before the widespread use of printing, and of course long before inventions like photography and television, few people knew what their king or queen looked like. Official copies of their portrait would be made to be given to important people around the country. Even nowadays, kings and queens are usually painted many times during their lives. They may be shown in ceremonial robes, military costume or less formal wear.

Which king or queen's portrait did you find?........................

....

What kind of clothes were worn for the portrait?...............

....Score **30**

Rembrandt: Equestrian Portrait

EQUESTRIAN PORTRAIT

A portrait of someone on horseback is called an equestrian portrait. Kings and queens are sometimes shown in this way, and so are soldiers, ladies and gentlemen and even children.

What sort of person was riding the horse in your equestrian portrait?..

Was it larger than life, smaller than life or about life size? ....

Was the horse standing still, or in action? ....

What colour was the horse? ....Score **30**

11

Landseer: Dignity and Impudence

ANIMAL PAINTINGS

The proud owner of a particularly fine horse, cow, dog, cat, parrot or other animal might have its picture painted. Two British painters, George Stubbs and Edwin Landseer, were both famous for their paintings of animals, but you will find work by other artists as well. On the front cover and p.3 is a beautiful painting of a cheetah by Stubbs, but to score points in this section your picture must have *no* humans in it!

What animal (or animals) did your painting show?..........

What was the title of the picture?.........................

....Score **30**

Hobbema: A Woody Landscape with a Cottage

LANDSCAPE

A painting of countryside is called a landscape. Very often these used to be painted indoors, and the artist would use sketches he had made out of doors to help him. He might add things, or leave something out of the real scene, to make the picture look better. Landscapes were particularly popular with British artists around 200 years ago, but you will find earlier ones from other countries too.

Was your landscape flat or hilly?...............................

What was the weather like?...............................

Who was the artist?...............................

What was the picture called?...............................

...............................Score **10**

Constable: Sketch for Hadleigh Castle

LANDSCAPE WITH RUINS

For a very long time it was fashionable for artists to visit Italy. They were interested in the ways the ancient Romans had lived, and they studied the ruins of Roman buildings. Sometimes they put ruins into their landscapes. You may score your points for a landscape with any sort of ruined building in it.

What sort of ruined building did your landscape show?..

Were there any people in the painting? If so, say about how many...................................... Score **10**

Rubens: Rainbow Landscape

LANDSCAPE WITH ANIMALS

Some landscapes are full of domestic animals, such as herds of cows, flocks of sheep, and so on. To score your points there must be more than four animals in your picture.

How many kinds of animals were there?

What were they?

Were there any people in the picture? If so, say what they were doing Score **10**

van de Velde: Three Ships in a Gale

SEASCAPE

In countries such as Britain and Holland, where a lot of their wealth came through sea trade, paintings of ships and the sea were very popular. You will find both merchant ships and warships in paintings, and some-times an important moment in history will be shown.

Was the sea stormy or calm in your seascape?......................

How many ships were there in it, if any?...........................

Was there any sight of land?.......................... ....Score **10**

Berckheyde: The Market Place at Haarlem

TOWNSCAPE

A townscape is a view of a town, shown more or less accurately. It will probably show a main street or town square, and one or two important buildings such as a church, palace or town hall. If people are included they will probably be small and insignificant.

Which town did your townscape show? ....

In which country is that town? ....

Were any important buildings shown? If so, say what

.... Score **20**

Seymour: A Kill at Ashdown Park

HUNTING SCENE

Look out for pictures of hunting scenes. They might be of a fox hunt, a boar hunt, a stag hunt, otter hunt, falconry or any other kind of hunt.

What kind of hunt did your picture show?..........................

Who painted it?..........................

Had the hunters caught anything? If so, say what...........

....

Do you think they were hunting for sport or for food?

..........................Score **30**

Ucello: detail, Hunt in a Forest

NIGHT SCENE

Paintings showing scenes at night are quite rare, but you will find a few if you look out for them. Your night scene might show the Nativity (see p.29), a landscape or seascape, or some other scene or story.

Look carefully at your night scene. What does it show?

Does it look like night time to you?

Is the moon visible?

What other lights are in the picture?

Score **60**

de Heem: Still Life with Fruit

STILL LIFE

A still life is a painting of a group of carefully arranged objects. You will find a wide variety of things in these pictures, such as fruit or other kinds of food, plates, glasses, fish and many other things. Score points for a still life with the following, and name the artist:

A lobster..Score **10**

Grapes..Score **10**

A seashell...Score **10**

Steenwyck: Still Life; an allegory of the Vanities of Human Life

VANITAS

The word Vanitas is Latin for vanity, and its use for this type of picture derives from a passage in Chapter 1 of the Book of Ecclesiastes in the Bible.

A still life may have a hidden meaning. For example, the objects in it might represent the five senses — sight, smell, hearing, touch and taste. One of the most popular types of still life is known as a Vanitas: the objects in it are there to remind us of death! Score your points for a still life with the following items, and name the artist:

A skull ....Score **50**

A snuffed-out candle ....Score **50**

van Huijsum: Flowers in a Vase

FLOWER PIECE

Some still life paintings are of vases of flowers. Quite often the flowers will be ones that bloom at different times of year from each other. So you may find spring and autumn flowers together in one vase. To do this the artist would paint each bloom as it came into season, so he would never have seen all the flowers together, except in his painting. You may even find that such a painting has more than one date on it!

Name the painter of a flower piece you saw with a striped tulip in it (these were very valuable flowers at one time)...
Name an insect or other creature you have seen included in a flower piece.. Score **30**

de Hoogh: An Interior Scene

SCENES OF DOMESTIC LIFE

Pictures of people at home are always interesting, as they show us what life was like in other times. You may find scenes in the kitchen, living room or other part of the house, and the people may be working or just enjoying themselves. Pictures of everyday life are sometimes called Genre Scenes (a French word, so it's pronounced 'zharnr'!)

What were the people doing in your genre scene?..........

....

Were there any children in the picture?............

Were there any animals?.................................Score **20**

Copley: The Death of Major Peirson

A SCENE FROM HISTORY

For hundreds of years artists have painted important moments in history. Usually the artist was not present at the event he painted, so he would have had to imagine what took place, using other people's descriptions to help him. This means that such a picture would show the artist's *idea* of what took place, rather than what actually happened. Look out for a famous battle on land or sea, a treaty being signed, or any other specific historical event.

What important event was shown in your history painting?..

....

Who was the artist?...Score **30**

Martineau: Last Day in the Old Home

A MORAL STORY

Some artists liked to paint a picture (or in some cases a series of pictures) in which a moral story is told. Like the story of a father who gambles and drinks away the family fortune, so the home has to be sold; or of a young person who goes to the bad and ends up in prison. You will find all kinds of unhappy stories of this type, some of which are sometimes made quite humorous by the artist.

What story did you find?..

....

....

Who was the artist?...
Did you find it amusing?...Score **40**

Cranach: Cupid Complaining to Venus

GREEK AND ROMAN MYTHS AND LEGENDS

Stories from ancient Greece and Rome have been popular for centuries. You will find gods and goddesses, heroes and heroines from these stories in many paintings. One of the most common goddesses to be shown in art is Venus, goddess of Love, and to score your points you must find a painting with Venus in it.

What was Venus wearing?..
What story did the painting show?...
....Score **40**

Mabuse: Adam and Eve

BIBLE STORIES

There are many stories from the Bible to be seen in paintings. Such pictures would often be done to hang in a church, but some would have been commissioned for private houses or palaces. I-SPY one of the first stories in the Old Testament: Adam and Eve in the Garden of Eden.

Was there a serpent (the devil in disguise) in your picture of Adam and Eve?..

Was there anyone else in the picture?........... ....

The devil tempts Eve to eat fruit from the Tree of Knowledge. Was there any fruit shown? If so, say what kind of fruit .... Score **60**

Duccio: The Annunciation

BIBLE STORIES

Another popular Bible story is that of the ANNUNCIATION: the Angel Gabriel visits Mary to tell her ('announce') that she is going to have a baby. You will find that the Holy Spirit is usually shown as a white dove near Mary. There will also be some lilies, a symbol of Mary's innocence, somewhere in the picture.

Where was the Dove in your Annunciation?.........................

What colour were the lilies?..

What was Mary doing as the angel arrived?.........................

....Score **20**

David: The Adoration of the Kings

BIBLE STORIES

Most Bible stories from the New Testament tell the story of Jesus. A picture of the birth of Jesus is called a Nativity, and the scene is often set in some sort of stable or ruined building. You will also find pictures showing the baby Jesus being visited by shepherds, or by the three Magi (the wise men from the East).

Did the baby Jesus have any visitors in your Nativity? If so, say who...

....

Were there any animals in the picture? If so, say what...

....Score **10**

Tintoretto: St. George and the Dragon

SAINTS

A saint is a person who has won a high place in Heaven by being exceptionally holy when alive. Lots of different saints appear in paintings, and, so that we can tell which saint is which, it is usual for each to be shown with some object that helps to identify him (or her). Saint John the Baptist is usually shown wearing a hair shirt or tunic, and he carries a lamb.

What was the name of the painting in which you saw him?..

....Score **10**

Look out for Saint George, the patron saint of England. He is usually shown in the act of slaying the dragon.

Was the princess he rescued shown in your picture of Saint George?..Score **10**

Crivelli: Altarpiece

SAINTS

Saint Sebastian was shot full of arrows by the Romans. He is usually shown almost naked, and with arrows sticking into him.

Who painted your picture of Saint Sebastian?...............
....Score **10**

Saint Catherine was to be tortured by being tied to a wheel. She was miraculously saved from this fate, only to be beheaded. She is usually shown in paintings accompanied by a wheel, though she may have a sword too. See the next page.

Who painted your picture of Saint Catherine?...............
....Score **10**

Lochner: Saints Matthew, Catherine and John

THE EVANGELISTS

The Evangelists were the writers of the four Gospels in the New Testament of the Bible. They are the Saints Matthew, Mark, Luke and John. There are several Saint Johns. This one is known as Saint John the Evangelist. Note the name of the artists who painted your Evangelist pictures.

Saint Matthew is shown with a little man with wings, rather like an angel..Score **10**

Saint Mark has a lion with wings..........................Score **10**

Saint Luke has an ox, and may be shown painting............
....Score **10**

Saint John has an eagle, and may appear holding a goblet with a snake in it..............................Score **10**

Crivelli: The Annunciation

SIGNS AND SYMBOLS

Sometimes artists put things in paintings for their symbolic meaning. (See p.21 for one type of symbolism in paintings). For example, if you see fruit in an unexpected place in a religious picture it is almost certainly there to tell us something. These meanings would have been familiar to the people living at the time when the picture was painted, but nowadays we often have to look them up.

I-SPY a pear, symbol of Jesus' love for mankind. What was the name of the picture you saw it in?.......................... ....Score **10**

I-SPY an apple, symbol of evil—evil and apple are the same word in Latin: Malum. Name the picture..................... ....Score **10**

Hilliard: An Unknown Man

SIGNS AND SYMBOLS

Flowers and other plants may have symbolic meanings too. Name the artists whose pictures you saw the following in:

Lily, symbol of innocence..Score **10**

Red carnation, symbol of pure love........................Score **10**

Columbine, symbol of the Holy Ghost................Score **10**

Violet, symbol of humility...Score **10**

Daisy, symbol of innocence....................................Score **10**

Rose, symbol of love..Score **10**

Dadd: The Fairy Feller's Master Stroke

FAIRY PAINTINGS

As no one has ever seen a fairy, you will find that artists have used their imaginations to create all sorts —from goblins and imps to pretty, delicate creatures with muslin dresses and wands. Fairy paintings are quite rare, and you may score points for any kind of fairy. Look for fairy paintings among pictures painted during the last century—the 1800s.

About how many fairies were there in your fairy painting? ....

Were there any humans in the picture? ....

Where did you find your fairy painting? ....

.... Score **50**

de Loutherbourg: The Shipwreck

A PAINTING OF A DISASTER

People have always been curious about disasters, partly because of the fear of being caught in one. Artists sometimes imagined what a disaster would be like and painted a picture of one. The sort of disaster you might find in a painting is a shipwreck, plague or volcanic eruption. You may also find famous disasters from the Bible, such as the Flood.

You may score your points for any type of disaster involving lots of people.

What was going on in your disaster painting?........................

....

Who was the artist?...

Did it look as if anyone was going to be saved?..................

....Score **50**

Raphael: An Allegory

A CARTOON

An artist often did a drawing on paper of the picture he was going to paint. He might then prick holes in the paper along the lines of the drawing, lay the paper over the canvas or wooden panel he was going to paint on, and dab powdered charcoal through the holes. In this way the outline of the drawing could be transferred from the paper to the painting surface. A drawing used in this way is called a CARTOON (from the Italian word for thick paper—CARTONE). The modern meaning of the word Cartoon is rather different, isn't it?

Look carefully at your cartoon. Can you see pin-pricks along the lines of the drawing? If so, the cartoon has been used.

Had your cartoon been used?..

Who was the artist?...Score **60**

Rubens: The Defeat and Death of Maxentius

AN OIL SKETCH

Another type of preliminary work is the oil sketch. The artist would do a small rough sketch in paints, in which he would work out how the picture was going to look. If he wished, he could then transfer this small design to a large canvas by squaring it up. He would draw a grid of small squares over the sketch, and a grid of large squares on his canvas. All he had to do then was to copy the sketch square by square. Quite often a busy artist would get his pupils or assistants to do this copying work for him.

What was in your oil sketch?..

Was it squared? If so, how many squares were there?..

What was the artist's name?..................................Score **40**

Hilliard: Self Portrait

MINIATURES

A painting that is small enough to be held in your hand is called a miniature. Miniatures are usually portraits, showing just head and shoulders; but you will find some full length ones as well. This was a convenient way of keeping an image of someone you loved, and you may find a miniature in a small case or locket so that it could be carried about or worn without getting damaged. The one shown above is full size!

Did your miniature show a man, a woman or a child?......

Was it a full length, or just head and shoulders?...............

Was the person holding anything? If so, say what...........

.... Score **20**

French School: The Wilton Diptych

A DIPTYCH

A diptych (say dip-tick) is a picture in two pieces. These are usually hinged, so that the diptych can be opened and closed like a book. It is most likely to be made of wood and to be painted both on the front and on the back. In a museum or gallery a diptych is usually shown open.

What was in the left hand picture of your diptych?..........

....

What was in the right hand picture?...

....Score **50**

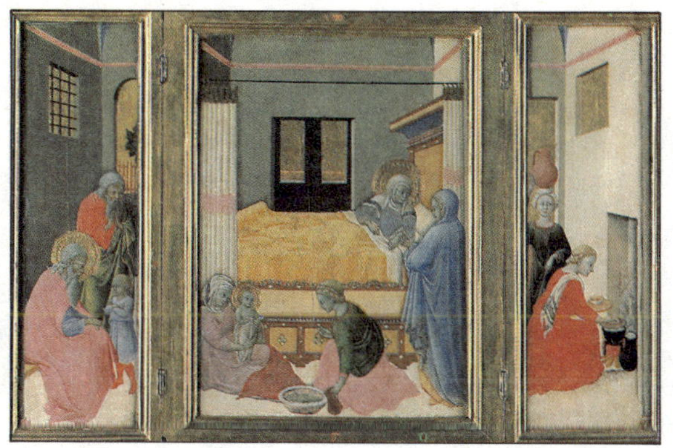

Master of Osservanza: The Birth of the Virgin

A TRIPTYCH

A triptych is a painting in three pieces: a main panel and two wings. Sometimes these are hinged. When the wings were shut they would cover the main panel. Often the paintings on the outsides of the wings would be in grisaille—that is painted only in shades of grey and white. A large triptych of a holy subject may have stood in a church, and might only have been opened on special occasions—for a service or feast day.

What was shown in the main panel of your triptych?......

Could you see the backs of the wings? If so, say what was on them..Score **40**

The Donor Portrait on page 6 is a wing of a triptych.

Venetian School: Altarpiece of the Virgin Mary

A POLYPTYCH

A painting in more than three parts is called a polyptych. It may or may not have hinged wings, and it may be of any size or shape. Each part is a picture in its own right, but its story will connect in some way with the other pictures in the polyptych.

How many parts did your polyptych have?........Score **50**

The stories in the pictures are usually about holy people, as this type of painting was often an ALTARPIECE (to go over an altar in a church).

Martini: Christ Discovered in the Temple

GOLD LEAF

In some paintings, especially in very old ones, you will find that the artist has used lots of gold. He will have used it for decorating people's clothes, for haloes, for the sky and in many other ways. The gold he used is real gold, beaten out into very thin sheets and then stuck on to the picture. Sometimes this gold leaf, as it is called, has worn away, and you can see the red-brown BOLE (a sort of clay) on which it was stuck, showing through.

What was the picture of? ....

Which parts were done in gold leaf? ....

....Score **20**

Studio of Botticelli: The Virgin and Child with St. John and an Angel

A TONDO

Tondo is the Italian word for Round. A circular picture is called a tondo, and it must also have a circular frame—see the inside front cover.

What was the subject of your tondo?.......................................

Who was the artist?.......................................

About how large was the picture?.......................................

Which country did the artist come from?.......................................

About how long ago was the picture painted?.......................................

Score **60**

Giulio & Penni: Saint Mary Magdalene Borne by Angels

FRESCO

A fresco is a painting done on fresh plaster (while it is still wet) on a wall or ceiling. As the plaster dries a chemical reaction takes place between the plaster and the paint, and the plaster becomes permanently coloured. Frescos are most common in Italy, where you find them on the walls of churches and palaces. However they were done in other countries too, and many fragments of frescos are in galleries and museums. Look out for a picture that has less bright colours and a matt surface. The label will usually tell you if the picture is a fresco.

Where did you see your fresco?...

Was it large or small?...

What subject did it show?...Score **50**

Verrio: detail of ceiling, White Closet, Ham House

CEILING PAINTING

Grand palaces or churches sometimes have paintings on the ceiling. These may be frescos (see the previous page) or they may have been done on wood or canvas and fixed up there. A few ceiling paintings have found their way into art galleries—where they are usually displayed on a wall! Look out for the people and objects in the picture being painted as if seen from below. You may score your points for a ceiling painting that is now in an art gallery or for one that is still in its original position in the building for which it was painted.

Who painted yours and where did you see it?......................

Score **30**

JOIN THE I-SPY CLUB

- All you need to join the I-SPY Club is to buy a Membership Book which includes the secret codes. Ask at your bookshop or newsagent.

- Tell your friends about I-SPY. Invite them to join and form a Patrol with you.

- Collect all the I-SPY books—and you'll have a wonderful library of your own.

- Write to me about any interesting discoveries you make. You may win a prize! Remember to enclose a stamped addressed envelope for a reply.

LOOK OUT FOR THESE I-SPY WITH DAVID BELLAMY BOOKS

AT THE AIRPORT	CAR NUMBERS
ARCHAEOLOGY	CARS
BIRDS AND REPTILES AT THE ZOO	CIVIL AIRCRAFT
	DINOSAURS
BRITISH COINS	GARDEN BIRDS
ON A CAR JOURNEY	TREES

AND MANY **MORE!** TO COME

ACKNOWLEDGEMENTS

'Adam and Eve' and 'Sir Edward Bonkil in Adoration' reproduced by Gracious Permission of Her Majesty the Queen.

'Miss Bowles', 'Rainbow Landscape', 'Flowers in a Vase' and 'The Defeat and Death of Maxentius' reproduced by permission of the Trustees, The Wallace Collection, London.

'Still Life with Fruit' reproduced by permission of the Syndics of the Fitzwilliam Museum, Cambridge.

Hilliard Miniatures—Victoria and Albert Museum, Crown Copyright.

'Cheetah and Stag with Two Indians'—City of Manchester Art Galleries.

'Elizabeth I'—National Portrait Gallery, London.

'Dignity and Impudence', 'Sketch for Hadleigh Castle', 'A Kill at Ashdown Park', 'The Death of Major Peirson', 'Last Day in the Old Home', 'The Fairy Feller's Master Stroke'—The Tate Gallery, London.

'Hunt in a Forest'—Ashmolean Museum, Oxford.

'The Shipwreck'—Southampton Art Gallery.

'Christ Discovered in the Temple'—Walker Art Gallery, Liverpool.

Ceiling Painting in the White Closet at Ham House, Richmond, Surrey—National Trust.

The remainder—The National Gallery, London.

Rear Cover—van de Velde the younger: 'The Resolution in a Gale' (detail), National Maritime Museum, Greenwich and 'Shell Times' for David Bellamy's photograph on p 2.
Series Editor Anthony Maynard.

Published by Ravette Limited, 12 Star Road, Partridge Green, Horsham, West Sussex RH13 8RA © Ravette Ltd. 1983. Printed in Italy (KEL)
ISBN 0-906710-26-X